LIFE CYCLES OF MARINE ANIMALS

EMPEROR PENGUINS

Michael Molnar

A+

This edition first published in 2012 in the United States of America by Smart Apple Media.

Smart Apple Media
P.O. Box 3263
Mankato, MN, 56002

First published in 2011 by
MACMILLAN EDUCATION AUSTRALIA PTY LTD
15–19 Claremont St, South Yarra, Australia 3141

Visit our web site at www.macmillan.com.au or go directly to www.macmillanlibrary.com.au

Associated companies and representatives throughout the world.

Library of Congress Cataloging-in-Publication Data has been applied for.

Publisher: Carmel Heron
Commissioning Editor: Niki Horin
Managing Editor: Vanessa Lanaway
Editor: Tim Clarke
Proofreader: Paige Amor
Designer: Tanya De Silva
Page layout: Tanya De Silva and Raul Diche
Photo researcher: Sarah Johnson (management: Debbie Gallagher)
Illustrators: Ian Faulkner (**7**, **8**); Muza Ulazowski (**12–25**)
Production Controller: Vanessa Johnson

Manufactured in China by Macmillan Production (Asia) Ltd
Kwun Tong, Kowloon, Hong Kong
Supplier Code: CP January 2011

Acknowledgments
The author and publisher are grateful to the following for permission to reproduce copyright material:

Front cover illustrations by Muza Ulazowski.

Back cover photographs: Shutterstock/Gentoo Multimedia Ltd (Emperor Penguins with chick), /Martin Fischer (Emperor Penguins on ice).

Photographs courtesy of: Auscape/Samuel Blanc-BIOS, **29**, /Fred Olivier, **26**; Australian Antarctic Division/Steve Brooks, **10** (krill); Dreamstime/Gentoomultimedia, **4** (top), /Lynne77, **4** (bottom); Getty Images/Bill Curtsinger, **5**, /Johnny Johnson, **11**, /Art Wolfe, **7**, /Norbert Wu, **9**; Photolibrary/Loïc André, **27**, /Greg Dimijian, **30**; National Geographic Stock/Minden Pictures/Norbert Wu, **28**; Shutterstock/William Ju, **6**; United States Antarctic Program/Joel Belluci, **10** (silverfish).

While every care has been taken to trace and acknowledge copyright, the publisher tenders their apologies for any accidental infringement where copyright has proved untraceable. They would be pleased to come to a suitable arrangement with the rightful owner in each case.

Contents

Read the story of one emperor penguin's life cycle in these pages.

Words that are printed in **bold** are explained in the Glossary on page 31.

Life Cycles of Marine Animals

Scientists believe that all life on Earth began in the ocean, hundreds of millions of years ago. Today, thousands of different animal **species** live in and around the ocean. No one knows exactly how many different species of **marine** animals there are—hundreds of new species are discovered every year. Although they share the same saltwater **habitat**, all marine animals grow and change differently over time. Each species has its own unique life cycle.

Life Cycles

All living things have a life cycle. An animal's life cycle begins when it is born and is completed when it has young of its own. During their life cycles, different species grow and change in different ways. Everything an animal does throughout its life cycle happens so that it can survive long enough to **reproduce**. Without this circle of life, all living things would become **extinct**.

The life cycles of marine animals can be as different as the animals themselves.

Emperor Penguins

To survive in some of the coldest and most dangerous places on Earth, emperor penguins have developed a unique life cycle.

Swimming Birds

Emperor penguins are large flightless birds. They do not need to fly, as they are great swimmers. Like other birds, emperor penguins lay eggs and look after their chicks once they have hatched.

Living Together

Emperor penguins gather together in large groups called **colonies** to feed and **breed**. By living together and helping each other, emperor penguins have a better chance of surviving and completing their life cycles.

When they swim, emperor penguins look like they are flying underwater.

What Do Emperor Penguins Look Like?

Emperor penguins are the largest of all the different species of penguins. They are birds with coloured feathers and have **evolved** short wings to help them swim.

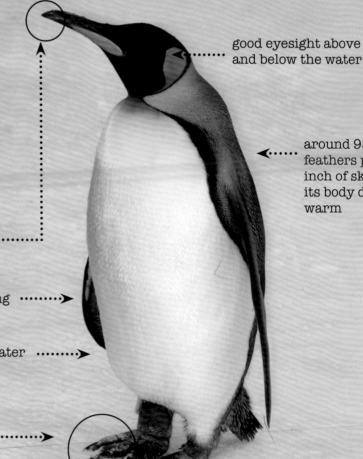

good eyesight above and below the water

around 95 waterproof feathers per square inch of skin, to keep its body dry and warm

long, thin beak for catching **prey** ....

short wings for swimming ....→

streamlined body to glide through the water ....→

webbed feet for swimming ....→

VITAL STATISTICS

Size: more than 47 inches (120 cm) tall
Weight: up to 88 pounds (40 kg)

Color: gray back, black head, white belly, yellow and orange under the chin and around the ears

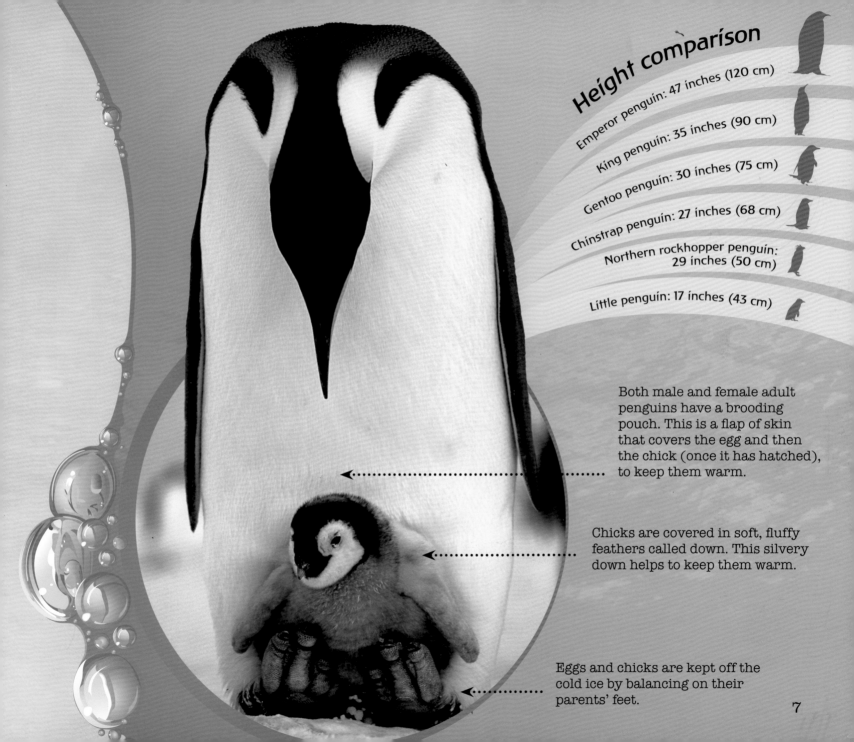

Emperor penguin: 47 inches (120 cm)

King penguin: 35 inches (90 cm)

Gentoo penguin: 30 inches (75 cm)

Chinstrap penguin: 27 inches (68 cm)

Northern rockhopper penguin:
29 inches (50 cm)

Little penguin: 17 inches (43 cm)

Both male and female adult penguins have a brooding pouch. This is a flap of skin that covers the egg and then the chick (once it has hatched), to keep them warm.

Chicks are covered in soft, fluffy feathers called down. This silvery down helps to keep them warm.

Eggs and chicks are kept off the cold ice by balancing on their parents' feet.

7

Where Do Emperor Penguins Live?

Emperor penguins live around Antarctica, in some of the coldest places on Earth. For several months of the year, there is no sunlight and temperatures can fall to minus 120 degrees Fahrenheit (minus 50 degrees Celsius). Some penguins never set foot on land, spending their entire lives in the ocean or on floating sea ice.

Emperor penguins are only found around the continent of Antarctica.

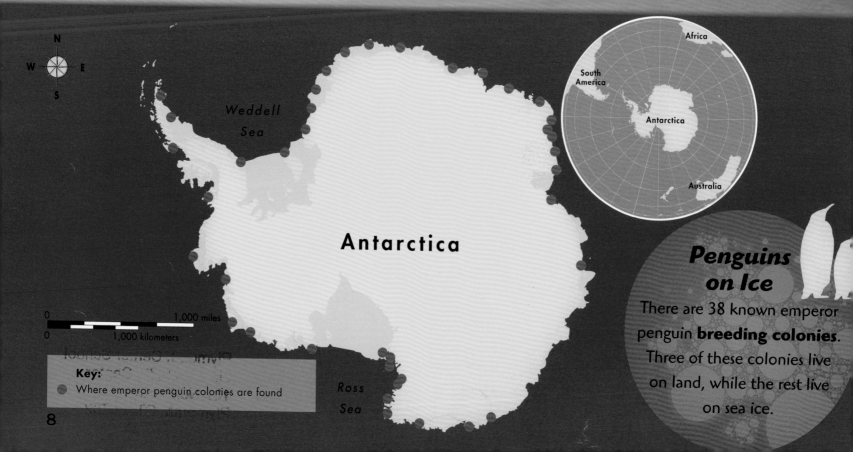

N
W — E
S

Weddell Sea

Africa
South America
Antarctica
Australia

Antarctica

0 — 1,000 miles
0 — 1,000 kilometers

Key:
Where emperor penguin colonies are found

Ross Sea

Penguins on Ice

There are 38 known emperor penguin **breeding colonies**. Three of these colonies live on land, while the rest live on sea ice.

Habitats

During their life cycle, emperor penguins spend time in different **habitats**. They are born and breed mainly on **fast ice**. Penguins can hunt underwater. They spend their summers feeding in the open ocean or along cracks in the sea ice.

Migration

Every year thousands of emperor penguins **migrate** from the open ocean to breeding colonies on the ice around Antarctica. It can take the penguins many days to cross the ice. The penguins must make this journey several times a year to bring their chicks food.

Heading South

While other penguin species are heading north to avoid the cold Antarctic winter, emperor penguins head south and begin breeding.

Emperor penguin breeding colonies can be located more than 60 miles (100 km) from open water.

What Do Emperor Penguins Eat?

Emperor penguins are **carnivores** that eat small fish, squid and krill. They can go a long time without food. Males can survive more than 120 days without eating!

Diving for Food

Emperor penguins are the deepest diving birds in the world. They can dive more than 1,600 feet (500 m) deep when chasing fish and squid. They can hold their breath for more than 20 minutes.

Foods that Emperor Penguins Eat

Antarctic krill

Antarctic silverfish

Glacial squid

How Much Do They Eat?

Emperor penguins can eat up to 13 pounds (6 kg) of food per day. This is nearly one fifth of their body weight!

Hunting Under the Ice

Emperor penguins dive into the water and swim down several metres under the ice. They look for the dark shape of a fish against the light colour of the ice above. When they spot a fish, they race up and grab it, before swimming back down to watch for more fish.

Hunting in Groups

By hunting as a group, emperor penguins can help each other find schools of fish and then work together to catch them. Penguins also hunt in groups for safety. They can look out for **predators** such as killer whales and seals.

Emperor penguins are great swimmers. They hunt together in groups to catch small fish, squid, and krill.

Weight Loss

Male penguins do not eat for about 120 days while they are mating and guarding their eggs. During this time they can lose more than half of their body weight.

THE LIFE CYCLE OF AN EMPEROR PENGUIN

Emperor penguins have a very unique life cycle. To complete their life cycle they must travel hundreds of miles across frozen seas and survive some of the worst weather in the world.

1

An Emperor Penguin Hatches

Emperor penguin chicks hatch from eggs. Once they hatch, chicks must be kept off the cold ice by resting on the feet of their parents. If a chick was to fall onto the ice, it would only survive for a few minutes. Chicks are fed by both their mother and father. The parents take turns hunting at sea, then return to feed their chick by **regurgitating** food into its mouth.

5

Laying and Caring for an Egg

After mating, a female emperor penguin lays a single egg. After laying the egg, the female carefully passes it to her male partner. The male will guard the egg and keep it warm until it hatches in about two months. The female returns to the ocean to feed until the chick hatches.

Alone on the Ice

When chicks are big enough to survive the cold on their own, they can be left in large groups. Both parents then leave to find food. If the weather gets too cold, the chicks huddle together for warmth. The feathers that cover the chicks are not waterproof. The chicks must grow new waterproof feathers before they can swim and hunt for their own food.

Learning to Swim

Once the young penguins have grown their waterproof feathers they can swim and find their own food. They can easily catch small fish, squid, and krill.

Finding a Mate

To find a **mate**, adult penguins must march many miles across frozen sea ice to breeding colonies around Antarctica. It can take them several days to make the journey. At the breeding colony they can find a mate and lay their eggs.

13

A young emperor penguin **hatches from an egg** that is balanced on her father's feet. The ice is too cold for her to stand on, so she is **kept warm** by a flap of skin under her father's belly.

She is hungry and cries for food. Even though her father has not eaten for four months, he feeds her by regurgitating an oily liquid into her mouth. Soon, her mother will return from the ocean.

When the mother returns, the father passes the chick to her. Moving the chick from one set of feet to the other is a tricky job! If the chick falls onto the ice, she will freeze to death in minutes. This time, all goes well.

Her mother has been feeding at sea for the last two months. Opening her mouth, she **feeds the chick with digested fish** she has caught.

Time for Sleep

Male penguins do nothing but care for their egg for two months before it hatches. To conserve energy they can sleep up to 20 hours a day.

It is now her father's turn to feed. He **leaves the chick with her mother** and makes the long walk back to open water.

Three weeks later, the young penguin's father returns, fat from eating fish and squid. The parents take turns looking after the chick. She must put on a thick layer of fat before she can be left alone in the freezing Antarctic weather.

Fat for Warmth

Emperor penguins can have a layer of fat up to 1.2 inches (3 cm) thick under their skin. This fat helps to keep them warm.

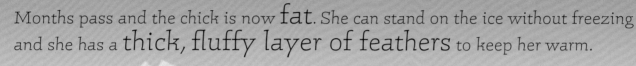

Months pass and the chick is now **fat**. She can stand on the ice without freezing and she has a **thick, fluffy layer of feathers** to keep her warm.

Both of her parents leave to find food, knowing that she will not freeze without them. **All the chicks stay together** while their parents leave to find food.

17

Late one afternoon, the clouds roll in. Suddenly a fierce wind begins to blow. The temperature drops and the emperor penguin chick starts to feel the cold. Her only chance to survive the storm is to huddle together with the other chicks.

They form a large circle to shelter from the freezing wind. The chicks stay huddled together for hours until the sky finally clears. By working together the chicks have survived

The chick's mother returns from the sea. She feeds the chick as much as she can before returning to the sea once again.

As time passes, the chick grows until she is almost the size of her parents. The days are getting longer and the sea ice is melting. She is almost ready to join her parents in the open ocean.

Vocal Calls

Chicks and their parents use their voices to find each other. Chicks also use calls to beg their parents for food.

19

Before she can swim, the emperor penguin chick must grow new waterproof feathers. Once her new feathers have grown she is ready to take on the cold and dangerous Antarctic waters.

Standing on the edge of the ice, the chick looks out over the ocean.

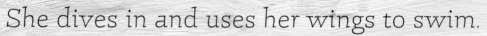

She dives in and uses her wings to swim. She is clumsy at first, but after a little practice she soon becomes a great swimmer. This will help her to survive.

One day, the young penguin is feeding on a school of fish when she sees a leopard seal closing in behind her. She zigs and zags, but she cannot get away—the seal is very fast. The penguin's **only chance** is to get back onto the ice. She races back to the ice pack.

Without slowing, she leaps from the water and slides across the ice. The seal can also move about on the ice, but is too slow to catch the penguin out of the water. The young penguin is **safe for now, but she must return to the ocean to feed.**

21

As time passes, the young emperor penguin becomes a better swimmer. She can dive more than 1,600 feet (500 m) deep to catch squid. She is fast enough to catch even the quickest little fish. She grows fat, hunting and feeding in the Antarctic waters. It is almost time for her to find a mate.

At four years old, she returns to her breeding colony. It is the winter and more sea ice has formed. The young penguin has to walk nearly 60 miles (100 km) across the ice to reach the colony.

After days of walking, she arrives to see hundreds of emperor penguins gathered together.

22

The male penguins put their beak down against their chest and make their loud mating call. One of the male penguins approaches the female. He repeats his call. She responds by lifting her head. She has found her mate.

The pair follows each other around the colony. They mate soon after and a single egg inside the female is **fertilized**. The two stay together until the female is ready to lay her egg. 23

A few weeks later, the emperor penguin lays her egg. She keeps it off the cold ice by balancing it on her feet. The penguin has not eaten for months and her **reserves** have run out. She must return to the ocean to feed. She passes the egg to the male and he balances it on his feet.

It is a long walk back to the ocean. As soon as she reaches the edge of the sea ice, she starts to search for **prey**. She has lost a lot of weight and needs to put it back on before she returns to her **mate**.

Two months later, the penguin returns to the breeding colony. She calls to her mate and listens for his response. She finds him and meets her newly hatched chick. Her life cycle is complete.

It has been four months since the male last ate, so it is his turn to feed. He passes the chick back to the female and makes his way to the ocean. The male and female take turns to feed.

It is up to both parents to keep the chick healthy so it can grow and continue the cycle of life.

Threats to the Survival of Emperor Penguins

Throughout their life cycle, emperor penguins face many threats to their survival. They must overcome these threats to **breed** and complete their life cycle.

When they are huddled in groups, emperor penguins take turns to be on the outside of the group, where it is coldest, and on the inside of the group, where it is warmest.

Freezing Winds

Emperor penguins must survive some of the worst weather in the world. Antarctic winds can blow at more than 125 miles (200 km) an hour and temperatures can drop lower than minus 120 degrees Fahrenheit (minus 50 degrees Celsius). During the worst weather, emperor penguins huddle together in large groups to keep each other warm.

Death of a Parent

Emperor penguin chicks grow very large and need to eat a lot of food. Young chicks also need to be kept warm. It takes both parents to feed and protect their chick. If one parent dies, the other parent will not be able to care for the chick alone.

Long Journeys

Emperor penguins breed on fast ice, hundreds of miles from the open water. Large expanses of ice can take days or weeks to cross. Parents need to walk to the open water to feed before returning to the colony to feed their chicks. If they take too long crossing the ice, their chicks can starve.

Large emperor penguin chicks need to eat a lot of food to survive, so both parents must work together to provide enough food. If either parent dies, the chick will not survive.

Predators

Three main predators feed on emperor penguins: killer whales, leopard seals, and southern giant petrels.

Killer Whales

Killer whales feed on adult penguins. Even penguins out of the water are not safe. Killer whales can swim into small icebergs to knock penguins into the water. They can also make waves that wash the penguins from the ice. Killer whales have even been known to jump right out of the water and onto the ice to grab penguins to eat!

Leopard Seals

Leopard seals feed mainly on sick, weak or injured emperor penguins. They usually wait near the edge of the ice for penguins to come past. The most dangerous time for penguins is when they are getting in and out of the water, as they can be easily grabbed by leopard seals.

Killer whales will sometimes swim into icebergs to try and knock penguins into the water.

Southern Giant Petrels

Southern giant petrels fly around breeding colonies looking for unguarded penguin chicks. Any small chicks that are left alone are easy prey for these large birds. Adult penguins are too large to be attacked by petrels.

Global Warming

The temperature of Earth's atmosphere is increasing because **greenhouse gases** are being released into the air. This is called global warming. If global temperatures continue to increase, the ice around Antarctica could melt. If all of this ice melts, emperor penguins will have nowhere to lay their eggs.

Emperor penguins need the sea ice to breed and continue their life cycles. If the sea ice melts due to global warming, emperor penguins will lose their habitats.

How Can You Help Protect Emperor Penguins?

To protect any animal we must also protect its habitat. As well as not harming emperor penguins, people must protect the oceans where these birds live and breed. Only then will they be able to survive and continue their life cycles.

Help Stop Climate Change

By sharing a car ride to school with a friend, turning off the lights when you leave a room, and not using much plastic or other throwaway items, you can help reduce greenhouse gases. **Recycling** and reusing things can also save energy and reduce global warming.

Join a Group

Many organizations have been set up to try and protect penguins and other marine animals around Antarctica. If people support these groups, there is a better chance that these animals and our oceans can be saved.

If Earth's temperature continues to rise, emperor penguins may be lost forever.

Tell a Friend!

Share your love of emperor penguins with someone else and show them how special these birds are. The more that people know and care about the survival of emperor penguins, the more they will want to help.

Glossary

breed   produce young

carnivores   animals that eat meat

colonies   groups of the same animals living together

evolved   developed over a long time

extinct   a species that is no longer alive on the planet

fast ice   floating sea ice that stays frozen most of the time

fertilized   started something growing

greenhouse gases gases, such as carbon dioxide, that contribute to global warming

habitat   a place where animals, plants or other living things live

marine   related to the oceans or seas

mate   when a male and female come together to produce young; partner

migrate   to travel a long distance from one place to another

predators   animals that eat other animals

prey   animals that are eaten by other animals

recycling   using something that already exists to make something new

regurgitating   bringing up food stored in the stomach back out of the mouth

reproduce   have young

reserves   stores of something that have been saved for later

species   groups of animals or plants with similar features

Index